FOREWORD

Sit me down on the sofa with a crochet project and before I know it, a few hours have passed. It's addictive to work in colours and patterns that will eventually give you a beautiful result. But be warned, you won't be able to stop!

Fair Isle knitting is already a well-known, traditional technique used to create multi-coloured patterns. But whatever we can knit, we can also crochet. In this book I will explain this crochet technique and you will soon see that it's not at all as difficult as it might seem at first glance. You can learn this technique fairly quickly, particularly if you are already a reasonably competent crocheter.

The vintage style fits with almost every interior: making old ways totally hip again is my passion and one that is reflected in the designs and styling. As luck would have it, there is a great shop on my street with a vintage flair, where I was allowed to take photos for my book. Projects include a throw, which is challenging, but wonderful to make. There is also a pouffe, a number of pillows, plant holders and many more ideas to work with.

I wish you good luck and lots of crochet fun!

With love,

Natasja

CONTENTS

THE BASIC TECHNIQUES

CHAINS (CH)

Start by making a slip knot. Yarn over and pull through the slip knot on your hook. You've now crocheted one chain. Yarn over again and pull through the chain on your hook. This is the next chain. Repeat this step as many times as indicated in the pattern. This is simply called a chain, or a series of chains.

DOUBLE CROCHET (US SINGLE CROCHET)

Insert the crochet hook into the second chain or the next stitch along from the crochet hook. Yarn over and pull it back through the stitch. Yarn over again and pull it through both loops. You've now made a double crochet stitch.

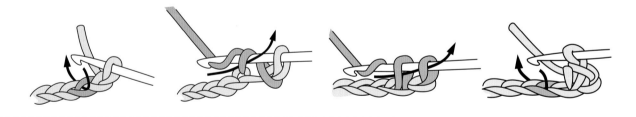

SLIP STITCH (SL ST)

Insert your hook into the next stitch. Yarn over and pull it directly through the loops on the crochet hook. This is a slip stitch.

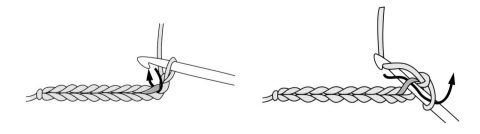

LOBSTER STITCH

Also known as crab stitch, lobster stitch is actually a reverse double crochet; you work a double crochet, but work it backwards. Turn your crochet hook and insert it into the last stitch you crocheted (to the right). Yarn over and pull it back through the stitch. You now have two loops on your hook. Yarn over again and pull it back through the stitch. You've now made a lobster stitch. Continue working to the right.

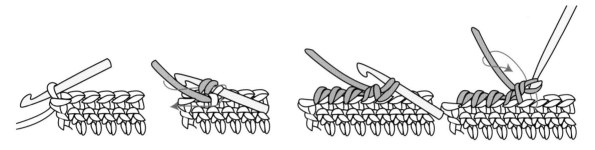

ADJUSTABLE RING

Also known as a magic ring, an adjustable ring is made to allow you to work the first round of stitches. First, make a large loop and work a slip stitch to secure the yarn to the large loop. Then work the requisite number of double crochet stitches into the ring, following your pattern. At the end of the round, slip stitch into the first stitch and pull the short yarn tail to close up the hole in the middle.

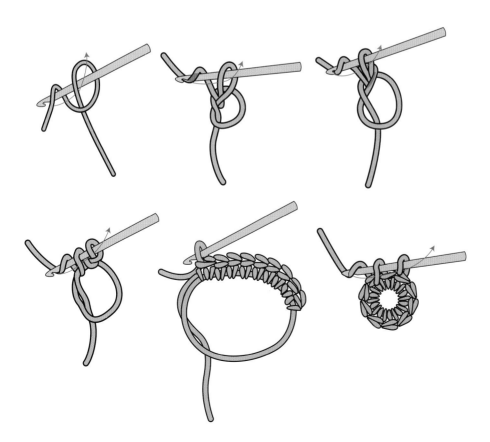

FAIR ISLE TECHNIQUE WORKSHOP

All of the items in this book are crocheted using the Fair Isle technique. This is a derivative of the mochila technique, or rather a combination of two techniques: mochila crocheting – a technique that has become well-known through beautiful crocheted mochila bags – and tapestry crocheting. The Fair Isle technique involves working with two or more colours. By crocheting with several colours, you can create beautiful patterns and figures.

To make the patterns stand out well, crochet into the back loops. This means that the stitches are placed directly on top of each other. It also helps to make sure that your pattern maintains its straight lines and is not skewed.

FAIR ISLE STITCH

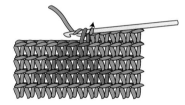  

Insert the hook into the back loop of the stitch from the previous row. Wrap the yarn round the hook.

You now have two loops on your hook. Now wrap the yarn round the hook...

... and pull through both loops to finish the stitch.

CHANGING THE YARN COLOUR

 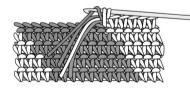 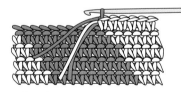

With the Fair Isle technique, several different colours of yarn are used. You work with one colour and allow the other yarn(s) to run alongside. Do this by inserting your hook into the back loop, underneath the carried yarn, then wrapping the current yarn round the hook and pulling it through in front of the carried yarn.

You now have two loops on your hook again. Yarn over with the new colour.

Pull it through both loops. You can now continue crocheting with the new colour, following the chart.

CROCHETING IN ROUNDS

When you crochet Fair Isle in a round or an oval, it is always worked in a spiral. This means that you continue to crochet the pattern and do not finish a round with a sl st. Because of the way this is done, the pattern is always staggered. It will be evident that the last stitch is higher than the first stitch of the round, particularly if you crochet a round using just one colour. Sometimes you can hide this by decreasing by one stitch and then increasing again (skipping). But this doesn't always work! It's all part of the technique, though, so don't worry about it too much

CROCHETING IN ROWS

If you use the Fair Isle technique in rows – for example, when making a blanket – you always crochet from right to left. After each row, a new row is fastened into the right (for left-handed people this will be the other way around). For each row, the carried yarn has to be continually fastened in.

TIPS & TRICKS

In Fair Isle crochet, a piece of work becomes stronger because the yarns you use are carried throughout the entire piece. In essence, what you're doing is crocheting around the yarn that you do not use. Those yarns are called carried yarn. The carried yarn tends to become visible between your stitches. Don't let it get too loose, but don't let it get too tight either! After about ten stitches, pull on the yarns to tighten them up and bring them into shape.

When a row has to be crocheted in one single colour, it is advisable to use carried yarn in the same colour. To do this, cut the width needed to crochet the row, and then allow for some extra on both sides. If you crochet with several colours, you will soon end up with the different yarn colours getting tangled up. To prevent this, it is important that you let go of all of the yarns every time you change the colour. Always take the new yarn from the ball towards you. This way, you can see precisely how the yarns run. If you keep doing this consistently, the yarn won't get tangled.

You can also use a shoebox to prevent your balls of yarn from rolling all over the place. Remove the lid, and make slits in the side of the box. Place the balls inside and run the yarn through the slits you have made.

ABBREVIATIONS AND CONVERSION CHART

UK crochet terms are used in this book. Since Fair Isle crochet uses one stitch only, in addition to chain stitch and slip stitch, reading the patterns is simple. Below are the most commonly used abbreviations, and conversions of UK terms into US terms.

UK	US
double crochet (dc)	single crochet (sc)
double crochet two together (dc2tog)	single crochet two together (sc2tog)
treble crochet (tr)	double crochet (dc)
slip stitch (sl st)	slip stitch (sl st)
chain (ch)	chain (ch)
chain space (ch sp)	chain space (ch sp)
repeat (rep)	repeat (rep)
stitch(es) (st/sts)	stitch(es) (st/sts)

BABY BLANKET

— DIMENSIONS —

90 x 60cm (35½ x 23½in) including 3.5cm (approx. 1½in) border

— WHAT YOU NEED —

Scheepjes Colour Crafter, or equivalent DK (8-ply/light worsted) yarn:
1 ball each in Ommen 1240 (pale pink/A), Pollare 2018 (black/B),
Veenendaal 1064 (brown/C), Lelystad 1026 (pink/D), Leek 1132 (coral/E),
Ermelo 1710 (beige/F) and Zandvoort 1218 (sand/G); 100g/300m/328yd

4mm (UK 8, US G/6) crochet hook

Stitch markers

You should have enough yarn left over from this project to make the Cuddly Bunny on page 22.

GENERAL

The blanket is crocheted using the Fair Isle technique as explained on pages 8 and 9. Each row is crocheted using two strands of yarn. For the carried yarn, use the two colours that appear in the row, or for rows in one colour, use yarn of the same colour. To do this, cut a strand of yarn to the same length as the entire width of the row, plus about 24cm (9½in) extra.

Crochet each row, and finish off at the end of each row. Right-handed people will start every row on the right-hand side, whereas left-handed people will start working from the left. Begin each row with 1 ch in the new colour. Add the second colour to this. Work 1 dc in the same stitch as the ch. Make sure that about 12cm (4¾in) of yarn remains on both sides of the blanket. It is a good idea to tie both strands of yarn firmly together at the beginning and end of each row, preferably with a double knot so that it can't come loose. This prevents large holes appearing when you crochet the border.

METHOD

Take yarn B and cut a length of about 1.2m (47in). This will be the carried yarn. Ch 100 and 1 extra ch. Start by working in the second ch from the hook. Add the carried yarn. Follow the chart to the end of the ch. Once you have worked all the rows of the chart, repeat it twice more.

BORDER

The border is worked in regular dc stitches, working through both loops of the previous stitches. All of the knotted yarn on the sides of the blanket is concealed within the border. Keep some stitch markers handy to mark the corners. Work 16 rows using the following colour scheme:

Rows 1 and 2: yarn D.
Rows 3 and 4: yarn C.
Rows 5 and 6: yarn F.
Rows 7–10: yarn A.
Rows 11 and 12: yarn F.
Rows 13 and 14: yarn C.
Rows 15 and 16: yarn D.

Start about halfway along one of the short sides of the blanket. With the right side facing, join in yarn using 1 ch and 1 dc in the same stitch.

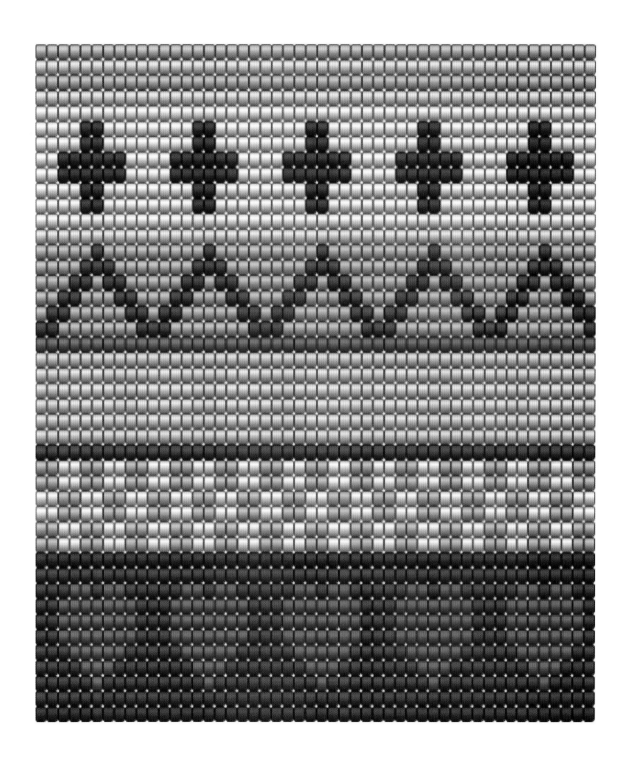

Crochet along all sides of the blanket. Along the long sides, work 1 dc into the side of each row. This can sometimes be tricky because of the many yarn ends that are hanging loose, but try to place a stitch between each yarn end and allow the loose yarn ends to hang to the back as much as possible. Work 3 dc in the corner, then place a stitch marker in the middle dc. Continue to work around the blanket, working 3 dc into the corner stitches, placing a stitch marker in the middle of these. End the round with a sl st so you don't end up with an ugly seam. Make sure you place a marker in the first stitch of the round to indicate the beginning of the next round.

Rounds 2–8: 1 dc in each st. In the corners, work 3 dc in the middle st of the corner from the previous round.

Round 9: 1 dc in each st. Do the same at the corners. Place the stitch marker back in the dc on the corner.

Rounds 10–17: 1 dc in each st. Reduce at the corners by working three stitches together as follows: yarn over and pull through the stitch before the marker, then the stitch with the marker, and again the stitch after the marker. Yarn over and pull through all three loops.

FINISHING OFF

Attach the edge to the wrong side of the blanket as follows: cut the yarn to approximately the same length as the border. Fold the edge neatly against the wrong side of the blanket, with the yarn ends tucked away in the border. Sew the edge in place with small stitches.

Crochet a decorative scalloped edge using yarn B as follows. Fasten in somewhere along the side of the blanket between the stitches, work 1 ch and 1 dc in the same stitch, 3 ch, skip 2 sts, *1 dc, 3 ch, skip 2 sts, 1 dc*. Repeat from * to *. Finish with 3 ch and 1 sl st in the first dc of the beginning of the round.

BABY'S ROOM STORAGE POCKETS

17

— DIMENSIONS —

Height including cuff: 24cm (9½in); width 20cm (7¾in)

— WHAT YOU NEED —

Scheepjes Catona, or equivalent 4-ply (fingering) yarn: 1 ball in Metal Grey 242 (A), and 2 balls each in Camel 502 (B), Peach 523 (C) and Rich Coral 410 (D); 50g/126m/138yd

2.5mm (UK 12, US C/2) crochet hook

Six wooden buttons 2.5cm (1in) in diameter

Three lengths of dowel 2cm (¾in) in diameter and 32cm (12½in) long

Two pieces of rope 1m (39½in) long

METHOD

Crochet three storage bags as follows: ch 48 and 1 ch for turning. Add all yarn colours and follow the chart. For this pattern, you will crochet around the chain (along one side and then down the other side). Work 48 dc to the end and repeat the chart on the other side of the chain.

Continue to crochet using the Fair Isle technique, following the chart. Work in a spiral, so ensure you don't finish the round with a sl st.

Weave in all yarn ends once you've completed the chart. No carried yarns are crocheted in the cuffs. Work 20 rounds in standard dc, working through both loops of the previous stitch. Fasten off and fold the cuff over. For the cuffs, use yarn D for 'Toys', yarn C for '&' and yarn B for 'Stuff'.

EARS (MAKE FOUR)

Round 1: make an adjustable ring using yarn A and work 6 dc.
Round 2: 2 dc in each st (12 sts).
Round 3: *2 dc, 2 dc in next st*, rep from * to * to end (18 sts).
Round 4: *3 dc, 2 dc in next st*, rep from * to * to end (24 sts).
Round 5: 1 dc in each st to end.
Round 6: *2 dc, dc2tog*, rep from * to * to end (18 sts).

Fasten off. Sew the underside closed and make three more ears. Place these on the side of the 'Toys' and 'Stuff' storage pocket just below the cuff.

TABS

For the tabs, crochet back and forth in the colour of the cuff as follows.
Ch 8 and 1 ch for turning.
Work 26 rows of 8 dc.
For the buttonhole, work 2 dc, 4 ch, skip 4 sts, 2 dc.
Turn work, 2 dc, 4 dc around the chains, 2 dc.
Crochet two more rows of 8 dc (30 rows).
Make a total of six tabs.

FINISHING OFF

Position two tabs per storage bag as follows. Place the storage bag flat. Count 6 stitches in from the sides. Secure tab from the seventh stitch. The second tab is placed on the other side, the seventh stitch from the side.
Position the buttons.
Drill holes in the poles at a distance of about 2cm (¾in) from the side.
Thread the rope through the first hole of a pole.
Put a knot at the bottom so the pole can hang.
The distance between the poles is 25cm (9¾in).
Measure out 25cm (9¾in), tie another knot and thread the rope through the hole of the second stick. Do the same for the third stick.
Repeat this for the other side.
Hang the storage bags on the poles and find the perfect place for them on the wall, by the bed or toy box, or on a door.

TIP

Embroider some whiskers on the 'Toys' storage pocket using yarn A.

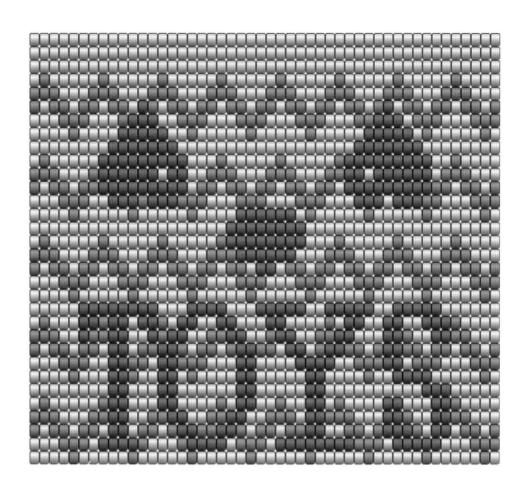

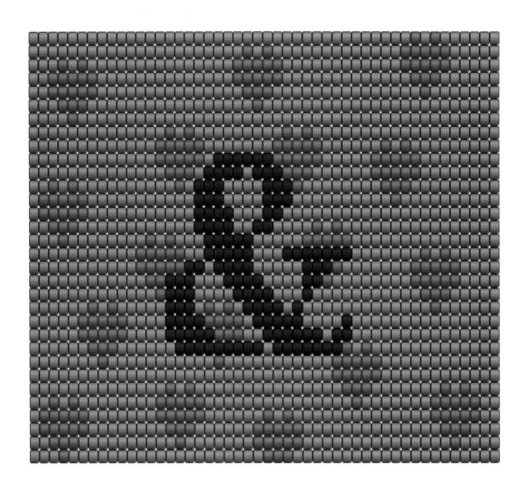

CUDDLY BUNNY

48 x 9cm (19 x 3½in)

Leftover Scheepjes Colour Crafter or equivalent DK (8-ply/light worsted) yarn in the colours that were used for the baby blanket (see page 11): Ommen (pale pink/1240), Pollare (black/2018), Veenendaal (brown/1064), Lelystad (pink/1026), Leek (coral/1132), Ermelo (beige/1710) and Zandvoort (sand/1218); 100g/300m/328yd

4mm (UK 8, US G/6) crochet hook

Toy stuffing

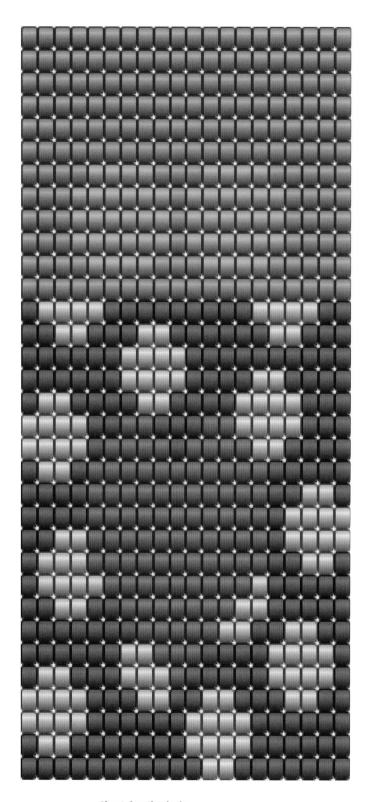

Chart for the body

BODY AND HEAD

The body and head are crocheted as one piece. Use yarns A, B and E for the body.

Using yarn B, work 20 chs and 1 extra ch.

Add the other two colours (for more information see pages 8 and 9). Use the Fair Isle technique to crochet 20 stitches following the chart. Start in the second ch from the hook. Repeat the same 20 stitches on the other side of the ch. Continue to crochet in the same way in a spiral. This makes the wrong side and the right side exactly the same. Change yarns after 21 rows.

Use yarns C and D to crochet the 12 rows of the head.

Weave in the loose ends neatly and lightly stuff the body and head.

LEGS

For the legs, use yarns A and B. Using yarn A, work
8 ch and 1 extra ch. Add yarn B and follow the chart,
crocheting in a spiral around the ch using the Fair Isle
technique. Starting in the second stitch from the hook,
follow the chart.
Repeat for the second leg.

TIP

Once you've crocheted the baby blanket, there are
probably a lot of cut-off yarn tails left over. These
can also be used as stuffing.

Chart for the legs

Chart for the arms

ARMS

For the arms, use yarns A and B.
Using yarn B, work 8 ch and 1 extra ch. Add yarn A and follow the chart, crocheting around the ch using the Fair Isle technique in a spiral. Start in the second ch from the hook.
Work according to the chart.
Repeat for the second arm.

EARS

For the first ear, use only yarn F.
Round 1: 2 ch, 6 dc in first ch (6). Continue using the Fair Isle technique in a spiral.
Round 2: 1 dc, 2 dc in next st, 1 dc, 2 dc in next st, 1 dc, 2 dc in next st (9 sts).
Round 3: 2 dc, 2 dc in next st, 2 dc, 2 dc in next st, 2 dc, 2 dc in next st (12 sts).
Round 4: 3 dc, 2 dc in next st, 3 dc, 2 dc in next st, 3 dc, 2 dc in next st (15 sts).
Round 5: 4 dc, 2 dc in next st, 4 dc, 2 dc in next st, 4 dc, 2 dc in next st (18 sts).
Round 6: 5 dc, 2 dc in next st, 5 dc, 2 dc in next st, 5 dc, 2 dc in next st (21 sts).
Rounds 7–9: 1 dc in each st.
Round 10: 5 dc, dc2tog, 5 dc, dc2tog, 5 dc, dc2tog (18 sts).
Rounds 11 and 12: 1 dc in each st.
Round 13: 4 dc, dc2tog, 4 dc, dc2tog, 4 dc, dc2tog (15 sts).
Rounds 14–20: 1 dc in each st.
Crochet the second ear in the same way using yarns B and C.
Work two rows in yarn C and one in yarn B alternately.

FINISHING OFF

Neatly sew together the openings of the arms, legs and ears. These are not filled. Secure the arms to the body, just below the head. Position the ears and legs. Embroider a face on the head.

CLUTCH BAG

— SIZE —

23 x 23cm (9 x 9in)

— WHAT YOU NEED —

Scheepjes Catona, or equivalent 4-ply (fingering) yarn: 1 ball each in Jet Black 110 (A), Bridal White 105 (B), Lime Juice 392 (C), Mercury 074 (grey/D) and Willow 395 (dark green/E); 50g/126m/138yd)

2.5mm (UK 12, US C/2) crochet hook

120cm (47¼in) length of chain

Two keyrings

Cork or fabric label (optional)

METHOD

Using yarn D, work 64 ch and 1 extra ch.

Start by working in the second ch from the hook, following the chart. Add the other four colours and crochet in a spiral, using the Fair Isle technique.

Work the chart twice around the ch. Do not make any increases. This will make it possible to crochet it all in one go. At the beginning, the work might curl a little, but just continue and, as you progress, it will stop curling.

There are two parts to the chart. The upper part is the flap section of the clutch bag.

After crocheting the entire chart, fasten off all yarns except yarn A. Work the last row as follows: 1 ch and turn the work. Continue to crochet on the inside. Work 1 tr in first stitch, 1 sl st into next stitch, *1 tr in next st, 1 sl st in next st*, repeat from * to * to end. Finish with a sl st in the tr at the beginning of the round. Fasten off.

FINISHING OFF

Attach both keyrings. Place them on both sides of the clutch just below the flap. Attach the chain to both keyrings. Fold down the flap. Make a braid of three lots of six strands of yarn that is about 50cm (19¾in) long. Fold this in half and tie a chunky knot at the ends. Fasten the knot to a keyring. Finally, attach a label to the flap to complete the clutch bag.

To work treble stitch:
wrap the yarn around the hook, insert into next stitch, wrap the yarn around the hook and pull through (3 loops on hook), wrap the yarn around the hook and pull through 2 stitches, wrap the yarn around the hook and pull through the remaining 2 stitches. The stitch is completed.

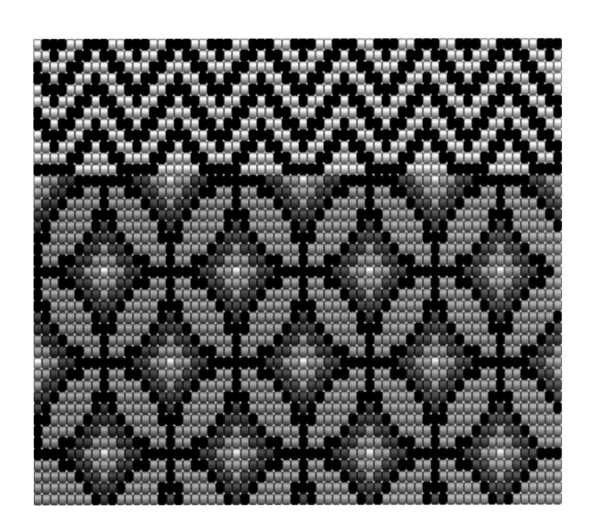

PLANT HOLDERS

— SIZE —

Height including cuff: 20cm (7¾in), diameter 15cm (6in)

— WHAT YOU NEED —

Scheepjes Catona or equivalent 4-ply (fingering) yarn: 3 balls each in
Jet Black 110 (A), Bridal White 105 (B) and Metal Grey 242 (C) and
2 balls in Lime Juice 392 (D); 50g/126m/138yd

2.5mm (UK 12, US C/2) crochet hook

Fabric stiffener

Label (optional)

PINEAPPLE PLANT HOLDER

Start by crocheting the base. This is worked using standard dc working through both loops. Use the same colour for the carried yarn as the one you use to work the base. In this example, yarn B is used.

Round 1: using yarn B, make an adjustable ring and work 8 dc (8 sts).

Round 2: 2 dc in each st (16).

Round 3: *1 dc, 2 dc in next st*, rep from * to * to end of round (24 sts).

Round 4: *1 dc, 2 dc in next st, 1 dc*, rep from * to * to end of round (32 sts).

Round 5: *3 dc, 2 dc in next st*, rep from * to * to end of round (40 sts).

Round 6: *2 dc, 2 dc in next st, 2 dc*, rep from * to * to end of round (48 sts).

Round 7: *5 dc, 2 dc in next st*, rep from * to * to end of round (56 sts).

Round 8: *3 dc, 2 dc in next st, 3 dc*, rep from * to * to end of round (64 sts).

Round 9: *7 dc, 2 dc in next st*, rep from * to * to end of round (72 sts).

Round 10: *4 dc, 2 dc in next st, 4 dc*, rep from * to * to end of round (80 sts).

Round 11: *9 dc, 2 dc in next st*, rep from * to * to end of round (88 sts).

Round 12: *5 dc, 2 dc in next st, 5 dc*, rep from * to * to end of round (96 sts).

Round 13: *11 dc, 2 dc in next st*, rep from * to * to end of round (104 sts).

Round 14: *6 dc, 2 dc in next st, 6 dc*, rep from * to * to end of round (112 sts).

Round 15: *13 dc, 2 dc in next st*, rep from * to * until end of round (120 sts).

Do not fasten off.

Strengthen the base with fabric stiffener. Leave it to dry thoroughly before proceeding.

Work the side in a spiral using the Fair Isle technique. Because you're not increasing any more, the work will increase in height. Add the required colours and work according to the chart.

Fasten off.

Using yarn C, work 20 rounds of standard dc working through both loops for the cuff. Finish with a sl st in the last dc of the previous round and fasten off. Weave in any loose ends.

Fold the cuff over and stitch on the label, and your first plant holder is ready.

The other two plant holders can be worked in exactly the same way.

CROSSES PLANT HOLDER

To make this, follow the instructions for the Pineapple Plant Holder on page 34. Crochet the base in yarn A. Use yarn D and work 20 rounds of dc for the cuff.

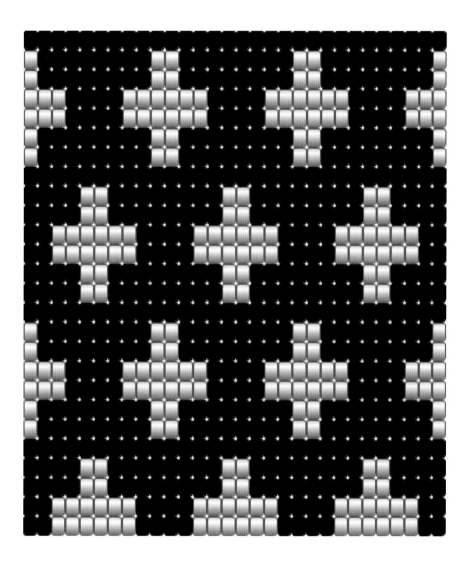

AMPERSAND PLANT HOLDER

To make this, follow the instructions for the Pineapple Plant Holder on page 34. Crochet the base in yarn C. Use yarn B and work 20 rounds of dc for the cuff.

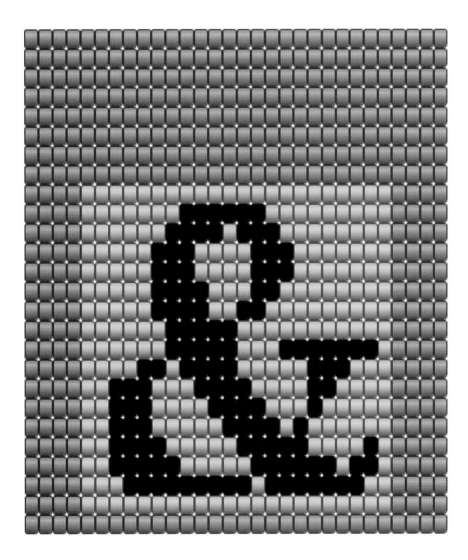

LARGE PLANT HOLDER

— SIZE —

Height 27cm (10¾in), diameter 26cm (10¼in)

— WHAT YOU NEED —

Drops Paris or equivalent aran (worsted/10-ply) yarn: 4 balls each in
Black 15 (A) and Off White 17 (B), 4 balls in Dark Beige 26 (C);
50g/75m/82yd

Two cork strap handles 35 x 3.5cm (13¾ x 1⅜in)

5mm (UK 6, US H/8) crochet hook

Fabric stiffener

GENERAL

Crochet the plant holder holding the yarn doubled and using the Fair Isle technique.

METHOD

The base is crocheted in a circle using the spiral method. The rows are therefore not finished with a sl st. Use two balls of yarn A and two balls of Yarn B.

Round 1: using two strands of yarn B, work 8 dc into an adjustable ring. Add the two strands of yarn A.

Continue to crochet as shown in the chart. Increase 8 sts per round until the base has 144 stitches. (There is more information on pages 8 and 9 about working in the round and the Fair Isle technique.) Flatten out the base and strengthen it with fabric stiffener. Leave it to dry thoroughly before proceeding.

SIDE

Continue to crochet without increasing. Use the Fair Isle technique and follow the chart, working in a spiral. There are 19 rounds. Note: continue to use the yarn doubled. To make sure the side is firm, add two more strands of yarn B. A total of six strands of yarn are now being crocheted: two strands of yarn A and four strands of yarn B.

Weave in all the loose ends once you've completed the chart and neatly tuck them away. Using yarn C, fasten it into the stitch after the last stitch of the previous round. To achieve a solid edge, use doubled yarn and two carried yarns and crochet 6 rounds in standard dc, working through both loops of the previous stitch. If you don't find the sides of the holder strong enough or if you want to prevent them from collapsing inwards, you can strengthen the inside with fabric stiffener.

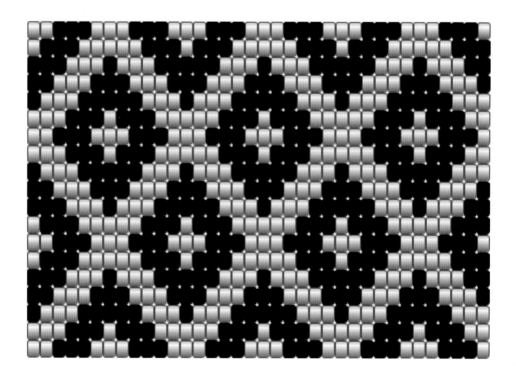

POUFFE

— SIZE —

Height 20cm (7¾in), diameter 54cm (21¼in)

— WHAT YOU NEED —

Rico Super Big Aran, or equivalent aran (10-ply/worsted) yarn: 1 ball each in Stone Grey 007 (A) and Ivory 001 (B); 400g/880m/962yd

5.5 (UK 5, US I/9) and 6mm (UK 4, US J/10) crochet hooks

Inner pouffe 50 x 20cm (19¾ x 7¾in)

METHOD

The pouffe is crocheted in two parts. Start with the top, which is crocheted in a circle using the Fair Isle technique.

TOP

Using the 5.5mm (UK 5, US I/9) hook and yarn A, make an adjustable ring and work 8 dc. Add yarn B and continue to crochet according to the chart. Always crochet using one carried strand of yarn. After 12 rounds, your work will be approximately 10cm (4in) in diameter. If not, adjust the size of the crochet hook. The top side should have a diameter of about 55cm (21¾in).

Please note: increase each round by 8 stitches, to a total of 256 stitches around the perimeter of the top.

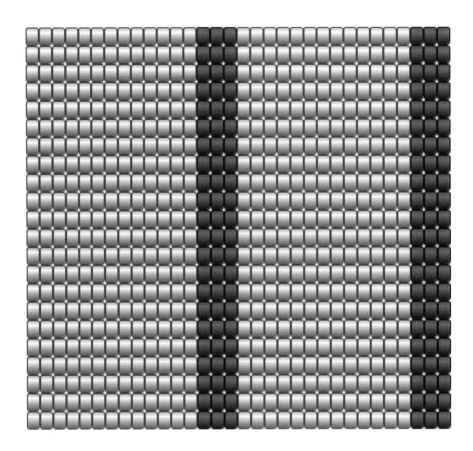

SIDE

Continue crocheting along the side according to the chart. Repeat this pattern of 32 stitches eight times across the 256 stitches. There are no more increases. Work yarn A into the first stitch of one of the star tips on the top side. The grey stripes then end up in a nice straight line downwards. Add yarn B and continue to crochet using the Fair Isle technique in a spiral. Crochet 22 rounds, following the chart. Check that the cover fits and work a few extra rounds if necessary. Fasten off.

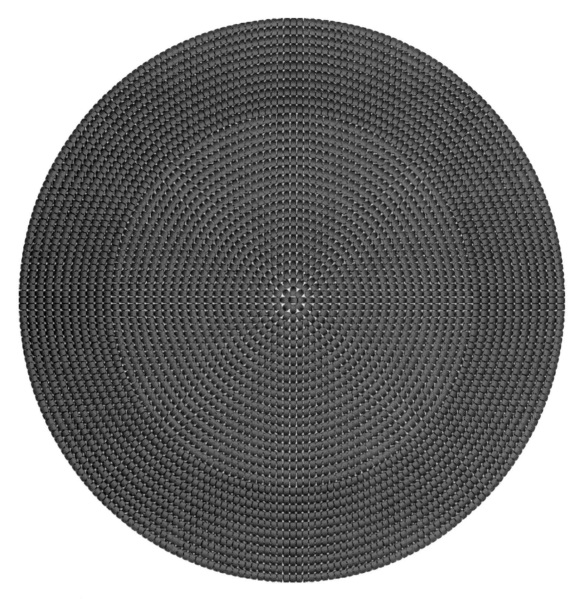

BASE

Crochet the base using two strands of yarn A. Take the large ball and create a second ball of about 50g. Use this ball as carried yarn. Crochet the base in yarn A in the same way as the top until you have created a diameter of about 55cm (21¾in).

FINISHING OFF

Crochet along the transition from the top to the side using yarn A doubled and a 6mm (UK 4, US J/10) hook, working 256 lobster stitches (see page 7). Fasten off and weave in the yarn ends. Pull the cover neatly over the inner pouffe. Attach the base to the side by working 256 dc.

PRETTY PILLOWS

— SIZE —

35 x 35cm (13¾ x 13¾in)

— WHAT YOU NEED —

Durable Cosy Fine, or equivalent DK (8-ply/light worsted) yarn, 3 balls in Mint 2137 (A), 5 balls in White 310 (B) and 4 balls in Black 325 (C); 50g/105m/115yd

4.5mm (UK 7, US 7) crochet hook

Two inner pillows 35 x 35cm (13¾ x 13¾in)

METHOD FOR CHEVRON PILLOW

Using yarn B, work 70 ch and 1 extra ch. Add yarn A.
Insert the hook into the second ch from the hook and work 70 stitches according to the chart, using the Fair Isle technique.
Repeat the same 70 stitches on the other side of the ch.
Continue to crochet according to the chart in a spiral. This makes the front and back exactly the same.
At the beginning, your work may curl a little. This will straighten itself out later on.
Fasten off when all the rows of the chart have been crocheted.

FINISHING OFF

Pull the cover over the inner pillow and sew the opening closed using tiny stitches. When sewing, work into the back loop only at the front and the front loop at the back of the cover, so the seam is not too thick.

BORDER

Use yarn C to crochet a border around the pillow as follows. Start at the top right of the cover (left-handed people should start at the top left).
Insert the crochet hook into the front loop of the front and the back loop of the back and work a sl st. Work a dc into the same stitch. Now crochet 68 dc, and work 3 dc into the last dc on the corner.
Continue along the side and crochet 52 dc. Work 3 dc into the corner.
Continue along the bottom and crochet 69 dc. Work 3 dc into the corner and 52 dc along the side.
Crochet 2 dc into the last stitch at the corner and using a sl st, join to the first dc of the beginning of the row.
Crochet a lobster stitch into each stitch (see page 7).

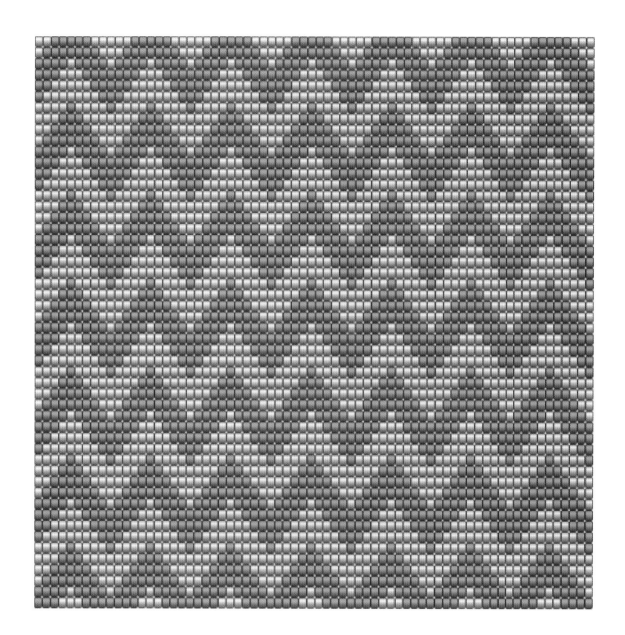

METHOD FOR CROSSES PILLOW

Crochet this pillow in the same way as you made the chevron pillow.
Using yarn C, work 70 ch and 1 extra ch.
The first stitch is worked into the second ch from the hook.
Work according to the chart around the ch.
Fasten off when all the rows of the chart have been crocheted.

FINISHING OFF

Pull the cover over the inner pillow and sew the opening closed using tiny stitches. When sewing, work into the back loop only at the front and the front loop at the back of the cover, so the seam is not too thick.

BORDER

Use yarn A to crochet a border around the pillow as follows. Start at the top right of the cover (left-handed people should start at the top left).
Insert the crochet hook into the front loop of the front stitch and the back loop of the back stitch and work a sl st. Work a dc into the same stitch. Now crochet 68 dc, and work 3 dc into the last dc on the corner.
Continue along the side and work 49 dc. Work another 3 dc into the corner.
Continue along the bottom and crochet 69 dc. Work another 3 dc into the corner and 49 dc along the side.
Crochet 2 dc into the last stitch at the corner and using a sl st, join to the first dc of the beginning of the round.
Round 2: work 1 ch and 1 dc into the same stitch, *3 ch, skip 1 st, 1 dc*, rep from * to * around the pillow. Close the round with 1 sl st in the first dc of the beginning of the round.
Weave in all loose ends.

TIP

Finishing your work with a personalized label can be a really nice touch!

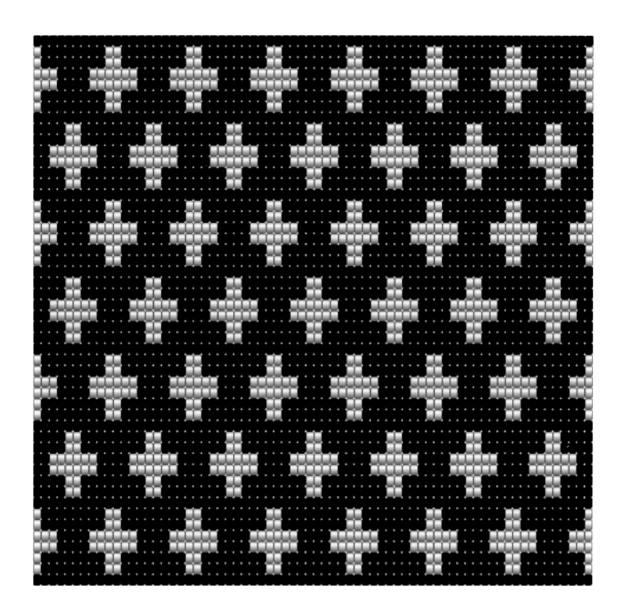

THROW

— SIZE —

185cm x 115cm (73 x 45¼in) including 3.5cm (1⅜in) border

— WHAT YOU NEED —

Scheepjes Colour Crafter, or equivalent DK (8-ply/light worsted) yarn: 6 balls in Ede 1002 (black/A), 3 balls in Weert 1001 (white/B), 2 balls in Wolvega 1099 (grey/C) and 1 ball each in Delfzijl 1822 (lime green/D) and Goes 1820 (mint green/E); 100g/300m/328yd

4mm (UK 8, US G/6) crochet hook

Stitch markers

GENERAL

This throw is not only great to snuggle under, but is also a real eye-catcher for a Scandinavian-style interior design. These patterns are certainly not boring, and are actually rather addictive! Experiment with colours to create your own unique throw.

The throw is crocheted using the Fair Isle technique as explained on pages 8 and 9. Crochet each row using two strands of yarn. Take the two colours that appear in the row in turn. If you crochet a row in one colour, use the same colour for the carried yarn. To do this, cut a strand to the same length as the entire width of the row, plus about 24cm (9½in) extra for both sides. Make sure that about 12cm (4¾in) of yarn remains on both sides of the throw.

Crochet each row, and finish off at the end of each row. Right-handed people will start every row on the right-hand side, whereas left-handed people will start crocheting from the left. Begin each row with 1 ch in the new colour. Add the second colour. Work 1 dc in the same stitch as the ch.

It is a good idea to tie both strands of yarn firmly together at the beginning and end of each row, preferably with a double knot so that it cannot come loose. This prevents large holes appearing when you crochet the border.

METHOD

Using yarn F, ch 200. Do this loosely or use a larger crochet hook. Work 1 ch extra. Make your first stitch in the second ch from the hook. Add the second yarn colour to the hook and continue to follow the chart. Repeat the chart to the end of the row (four times).

BORDER

The border consists of standard dc, working into both loops of the previous stitch. All of the knotted yarn on the sides of the throw is concealed within the folded-over border. Keep some stitch markers handy to mark the edges. Start somewhere halfway along one of the short sides of the throw. With the right side facing and, using yarn A, make 1 ch and 1 dc in the same stitch. Put a marker in the first stitch to indicate the start of the row. Work dc along all sides of the throw. Along the long sides, work 1 dc into the side of each row.

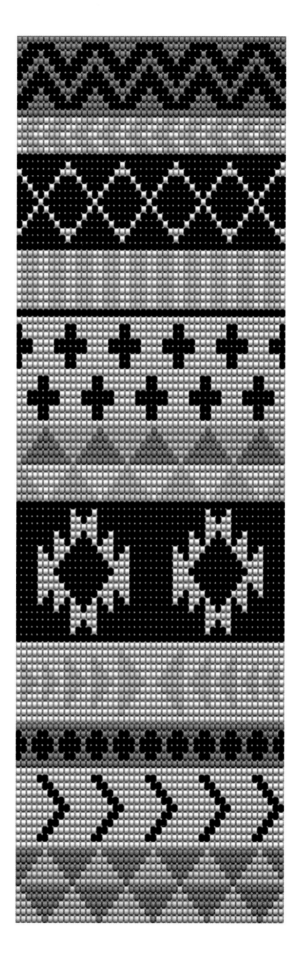

Chart continues on page 63

This can sometimes be tricky because of the many yarn ends that are hanging loose, but try to place a stitch between each strand of yarn and allow the loose yarn to hang to the back as much as possible. Work 3 dc into the corner, then place a marker in the middle dc. Do this with each corner. Continue to crochet around. Do not finish the row with a sl st, but crochet round in a spiral so you do not end up with a seam in your work. Make sure to mark each round with a stitch marker to indicate the start of the new round.

Rounds 2–8: 1 dc in each st. In the middle stitch of the 3 dc in each corner of the previous round, work 3 dc.

Round 9: 1 dc in each st, including the corners. Place the stitch marker back in the dc on the corner.

Rounds 10–17: 1 dc in each st. Reduce at the corners by crocheting three stitches together as follows: yarn over and pull through the stitch before the marker, then in the stitch with the marker and again in the stitch after the marker. Yarn over and pull the yarn through all loops. Place the marker into the newly made stitch to indicate the corner for the next round. Gradually, the border will start to fold inwards.

FINISHING OFF

Attach the border to the back of the throw as follows. Cut the yarn approximately to the equal length of the border. Fold the border neatly against the wrong side of the blanket, with the yarn ends tucked away in the border. Sew the border in place with small stitches.

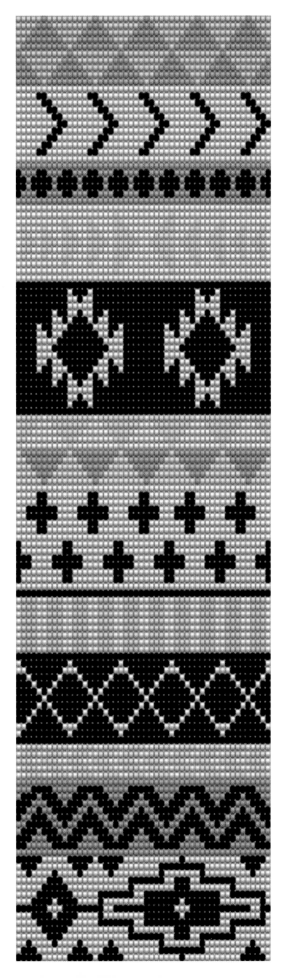

WALL HANGING

45cm x 32cm ($17\frac{3}{4}$ x $12\frac{1}{2}$in) diameter

WHAT YOU NEED

Durable Cosy Fine, or equivalent DK (8-ply/light worsted) yarn: 1 ball each in Black 325 (A), Ash 2235 (B), Grey Silver 2228 (C), White 310 (D) and Fine Honey 2179 (E); 50g/105m/115yd

4.5mm (UK 7, US 7) crochet hook

50cm ($19\frac{3}{4}$in) length of dowel

25mm (1in) wooden beads with large hole

Two screw eyes

METHOD

The wall hanging is crocheted using the Fair Isle technique (see pages 8 and 9 for more information).

Work with a minimum of three strands of yarn on each row. For a solid row of colour, cut three strands of yarn in the same colour, 40cm (15¾in) in length (the width of your work plus 12cm (4¾in) extra for each side). This will be the carried yarn.

Work 61 ch and 1 extra ch. Add the loose yarn to the hook as carried yarn and work 61 dc. Start in the second ch from the hook and fasten off at the end of the row.

Do not cut the yarn too short and make sure that there is enough on both sides to finish off. For a firm edge, securely fasten the loose yarn with a double knot. This ensures that the yarn strands do not slip and that the work on the side does not become frayed. Continue to work as shown in the chart.

Reduce each row by 2 stitches from row 30. To do this, start the row in the second instead of the first stitch and fasten off in the penultimate stitch.

Firmly knot and then cut off the loose yarn on the side as follows: lay the yarn strands flat and cut them evenly to the desired length. In the example, 2.5cm (1in) has been used.

TABS

Crochet three tabs 6 dc wide as follows:
Ch 6 and 1 ch for turning.
Work 14 rows of 6 dc back and forth.
Sew the folded tabs to the wall hanger with small stitches.
Thread the dowel through the tabs and determine the position of the screw eyes. Screw these in.

FINISHING OFF

Make a tassel for the bottom of the wall hanger as follows:
Take some cardboard, about 12cm (4¾in) wide. Take a ball of yarn in the colour of your choice, and then wrap the yarn around it about thirty times. Cut another piece of yarn, slide it under the yarn on the cardboard and tie a secure knot at the top so that the strands cannot fall out. Cut off the yarn at the bottom of the cardboard. Take a large bead, thread it over the knotted end, and attach it. Attach the tassel to the bottom of the wall hanging.

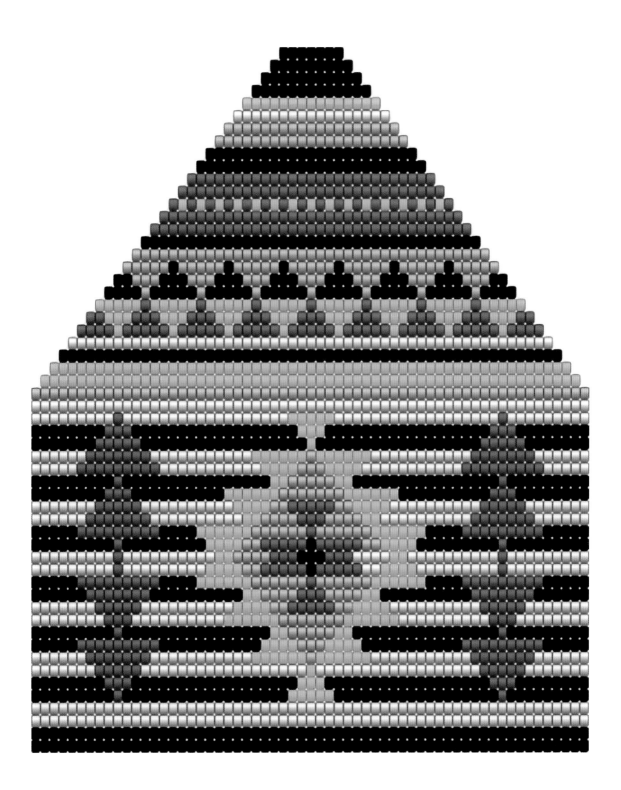

PASTEL PILLOWS

— SIZE —

Rectangular pillow: 50 x 30cm ($19\frac{3}{4}$ x $11\frac{3}{4}$in)

Square pillow: 40 x 40cm ($15\frac{3}{4}$ x $15\frac{3}{4}$in)

— WHAT YOU NEED —

Rectangular pillow

Drops Paris, or equivalent aran (10-ply/worsted) yarn: 2 balls each in Light Mint Green 21 (A), Light Light Pink 57 (B), Shocking Pink 06 (C) and Dark Beige 26 (D) and 1 ball in Black 15 (E); 50g/75m/82yd

Inner pillow 50 x 30cm ($19\frac{3}{4}$ x $11\frac{3}{4}$in)

4.5mm (UK 7, US 7) crochet hook

Square Pillow

Drops Paris, or equivalent aran (10-ply/worsted) yarn: 2 balls in Light Light Pink 57 (A), Dark Beige 26 (B), Black 15 (C), White 16 (D) and Light Ice Blue 29 (E); 50g/75m/82yd

Inner pillow 40 x 40cm ($15\frac{3}{4}$ x$15\frac{3}{4}$in)

4.5mm (UK 7, US 7) crochet hook

METHOD FOR RECTANGULAR PILLOW

Using yarn D, work 100 ch and 1 extra ch. Add the remaining colours. Insert the crochet hook into the second ch from the hook and work in a spiral, following the chart and using the Fair Isle technique. Repeat the chart on the other side of the ch. This makes the front and back exactly the same. In the beginning, the work will curl a little. This will straighten itself out later on. Fasten off when the chart is completed.

FINISHING OFF

Pull the cover over the inner pillow and sew the opening closed using mattress stitch, to make an invisible join, as follows. Take one stitch from one side and one stitch from the other side. Continue taking a stitch from alternate sides and pull the yarn gently after every few stitches. This makes the seam close up and the stitches disappear.

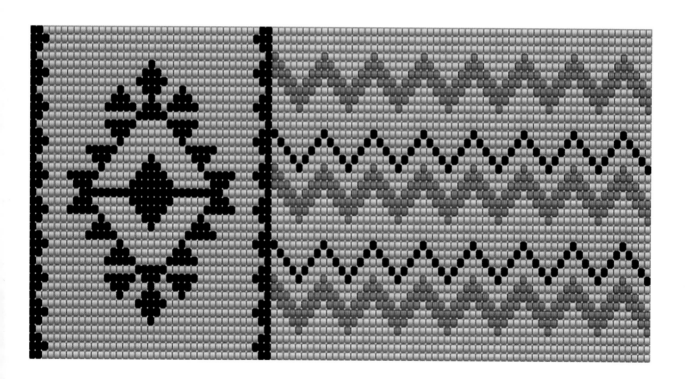

METHOD FOR SQUARE PILLOW

Using yarn B, work 78 ch and
1 extra ch.
Add the carried yarn.
Insert the crochet hook into the
second ch from the hook and work
in a spiral, following the chart and
using the Fair Isle technique. Repeat
the chart on the other side of the
ch. Continue to follow the chart.
Fasten off when the chart
is completed.

FINISHING OFF

Finish using the same method as for
the rectangular pillow.

MOCHILA BAG

Height 35cm (13¾in), diameter 24cm (9½in)

Scheepjes Catona, or equivalent 4-ply (fingering) yarn: 4 balls in Jet Black 110 (A), 3 balls in Bridal White 105 (B) and 1 ball in Fresia 519 (pink/C); 50g/126m/138yd

Scheepjes Colour Crafter, or equivalent DK (8-ply/light worsted) yarn: scraps in Luik 2006 (pink/D)

2.5mm (UK 12, US C/2) crochet hook

Fabric stiffener

Pompom maker

BASE

Using yarn A, make an adjustable ring and work 8 dc. Add another strand of yarn A, as well as a strand each of yarns B and C. Continue to work in rounds, following the chart and using the Fair Isle technique. Increase each round by 1 stitch eight times. Flatten out the base properly. Strengthen the base with fabric stiffener. This ensures that the shape is maintained and prevents the base from sagging. Let the fabric stiffener dry thoroughly before continuing.

The increases are indicated in green.
Repeat these for each round.

SIDE

Replace the carried yarn of the base (yarn C) with a strand of yarn A or B (so that you do not see the colour).

Continue to work without increasing. Use the Fair Isle technique and follow the chart. Crochet holes for the cord as follows:

5 dc, *ch 4, skip 4 sts, 21 dc*, repeat from * to * to last 16 sts, 16 dc. Work the next round of stitches into all stitches and 4 stitches into each ch space. Work over the carried yarns. This way they are neatly concealed and the holes for the cord are firm.

SHOULDER STRAP

Make the shoulder strap using standard dc, working through both loops of the previous stitch. Crochet two or more carried yarn strands to strengthen the strap.
Start by working 210 ch. Crochet 13 rows using the following colour scheme.
Rows 1–3: yarn A.
Rows 4 and 5: yarn C.
Row 6: yarn A.
Row 7: yarn B.
Row 8: yarn A.
Rows 9 and 10: yarn C.
Rows 11–13: yarn A.
Attach the strap to the inside of the bag using small stitches.

CORD

Take three strands of yarn, about 2m (79in) in length, and attach them to a door handle.
Take the ends of the yarn strands and tie a knot in them. Twist the yarn between your thumb and forefinger. It is important to do this firmly and evenly. The yarn must remain tightly tensioned while twisting. Keep twisting the strands of yarn until they are about to twist into each other. Take a heavy object, suas a pair of scissors or a bunch of keys, and let it hang in the middle of the stretched yarn. Always make sure you keep the yarn taut! Remove the other end from the door handle and stand on a chair (if necessary) in front of the long cord. It will start to rotate and will automatically become a nice, even cord. Wait until the cord is completely twisted.
Remove the object from the yarn: your cord is now ready.
Tie a knot on both sides.

POMPOMS

I used a large pompom maker and scraps of yarn D. Cotton yarn can be used if you prefer, but acrylic yarn has a fluffier structure, which gives a nicer shape to the pompoms.
Pull the cord through the buttonholes, then attach the pompoms to both ends of the cord to complete the bag.

A WORD OF THANKS

During the process of creating this book I received a lot of help and motivating words from many dear friends and family. Without their support, I could never have done it.

I'd like to thank a few people in particular. First of all, my dear, proud parents and children. Dad, Mum, Lucas and Kirsten. My sisters Susanne and Leontien. Thank you for your support!

Leonie Schellingerhout, friend and owner of Wolcafé, who encouraged me to write this book. I have benefited from your knowledge and experience. There are so many times I have needed your motivational words and support. Thank you for that.

Mariette, Patricia, Betty, Ria, Alice, Annemarie, Tertia and Gerdina. Thank you very much for trying out the crochet work and checking the patterns.

Thanks to Hanneke and Nicole for taking the beautiful pictures. You guys knew exactly what mood to create to achieve the end result I had in mind. Thank you.

I would also like to thank Pand 69 for opening up the shop where we were able to photograph to our heart's content. And to Marlies, for making your nursery available. And lovely little Saar, already a top model!

In addition to all the people who supported me, there are many friends and colleagues who have helped me along the way. Thank you to everyone!